やさしい英語で読む
世界のおとぎ話

# Contents
目次

## 本書の利用法
06

## ロバと店主 *The Donkey and the Shopkeeper*
09

## 枝の束 *The Bundle of Sticks*
15

## キツネとカラス *The Fox and the Crow*
21

## 裸の王様 *The Emperor's New Clothes*
27

## 農夫の宝物 The Farmer's Treasure　33

## ワシと農夫 The Eagle and the Farmer　39

## 農夫とロバ The Farmer and the Donkey　45

## 北風と太陽 The Wind and the Sun　51

## キツネとヤギ The Fox and the Goat　57

## ロバと ウマ *The Donkey and the Horse*     63

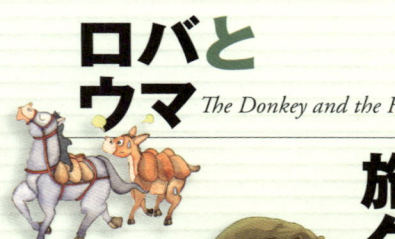

## 旅人と クマ *The Travelers and the Bear*     69

## 蚊と ライオン *The Mosquito and the Lion*     75

## のどの 渇いた カラス *The Thirsty Crow*     81

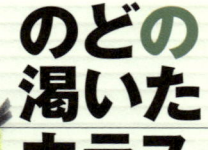

## 老犬 *The Old Dog*     87

## おばあさんと 医者 *The Old Woman and the Doctor*     93

# 高慢なサギ
*The Proud Heron*　99

# 守銭奴
*The Man Who Loved Money*　105

# 危険信号
*Danger Signs*　111

# 池のシカ
*The Deer at the Pond*　117

# 漁師と小さな魚
*The Fisherman and the Little Fish*　123

# Index
129

# 本書の利用法

> CDのトラック番号がここに示されています。CD14・15の場合は、CDのTrack 14とTrack15"ということです。

There once was a farmer who wanted to buy a donkey. He wanted a hardworking one that could help him on his farm. He went to a market and saw one that looked perfect.❶

"May I try out this donkey for a day or two?" asked the farmer. "If he is hardworking, I will pay❷ you a good price."❸

"Of course you may," said the seller. ❹ "I'm sure that he will please you." The farmer thanked the seller and took the donkey back to his farm.

### VOCABULARY

1. **perfect** adj. 申し分がない
2. **pay** v. (pay-paid-paid) 支払う
3. **price** n. 値段
4. **seller** n. 売主

*The Farmer and the Donkey* 農夫とロバ | 47

> ここには、物語の中で使われている語彙を取り上げています。物語を読む際に、活用してください。

> 品詞の表記について
> n.     名詞
> adj.   形容詞
> v.     動詞
> adv.   副詞
> prep.  前置詞

6

▶ **本書は、誰もが知っているお話を含めた20の世界のおとぎ話が収録されています。
1つのお話はイラスト、日本語訳を含めて6ページで構成されており、
手軽に読み進めることができます。**

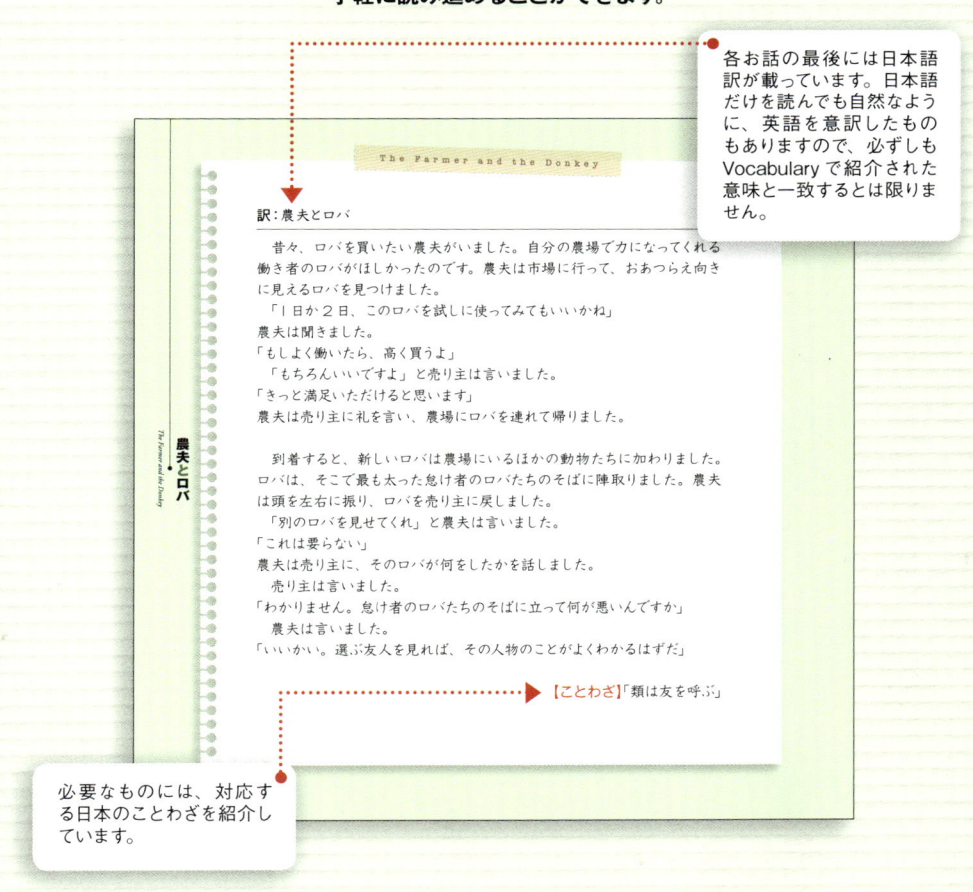

各お話の最後には日本語訳が載っています。日本語だけを読んでも自然なように、英語を意訳したものもありますので、必ずしもVocabularyで紹介された意味と一致するとは限りません。

The Farmer and the Donkey

### 訳：農夫とロバ

　昔々、ロバを買いたい農夫がいました。自分の農場で力になってくれる働き者のロバがほしかったのです。農夫は市場に行って、おあつらえ向きに見えるロバを見つけました。
「1日か2日、このロバを試しに使ってみてもいいかね」
農夫は聞きました。
「もしよく働いたら、高く買うよ」
　「もちろんいいですよ」と売り主は言いました。
「きっと満足いただけると思います」
農夫は売り主に礼を言い、農場にロバを連れて帰りました。

　到着すると、新しいロバは農場にいるほかの動物たちに加わりました。ロバは、そこで最も太った怠け者のロバたちのそばに陣取りました。農夫は頭を左右に振り、ロバを売り主に戻しました。
「別のロバを見せてくれ」と農夫は言いました。
「これは要らない」
農夫は売り主に、そのロバが何をしたかを話しました。
　売り主は言いました。
「わかりません。怠け者のロバたちのそばに立って何が悪いんですか」
　農夫は言いました。
「いいかい。選ぶ友人を見れば、その人物のことがよくわかるはずだ」

▶ 【ことわざ】「類は友を呼ぶ」

必要なものには、対応する日本のことわざを紹介しています。

農夫とロバ
The Farmer and the Donkey

7

# 学習法

本書を使って英語の読解力や聴解力をアップさせるのに有効な学習法を紹介します。
お話を楽しみながら、英語力を上げるのに役立ててください。

## Step1
**Vocabulary をヒントにしながら物語を読む**

## Step2
**日本語訳で確認**

## Step3
**CD（英語）を本を見ながら聞く**

## Step4
**CD（英語）を本を見ないで聞く**

偶数トラックには英語で、奇数トラックには日本語で、
お話が収録されています。
用途に合わせて、CD を活用してください。

# ロバと店主

*The Donkey and the Shopkeeper*

A hardworking ❶shopkeeper drove his donkey to the market to buy salt.❷ On their way home, they had to cross a stream. The donkey was very tired, and he slipped❸ on a rock and fell into the water.

To the donkey's surprise, his load❹ was now much lighter. The water had washed away almost all of the salt. The shopkeeper took the donkey back to the market and bought even more salt than before. This time when they reached the stream, the donkey fell into the water on purpose.❺

1. **hardworking** adj. ☞ よく働く
2. **salt** n. ☞ 塩
3. **slip** v. ☞ 滑る
4. **load** n. ☞ 積み荷
5. **on purpose** ☞ わざと

*The Donkey and the Shopkeeper* **ロバと店主**

The shopkeeper saw through the donkey's trick.❶ He returned to the market and bought sponges❷ instead of salt.

When they reached the stream, the donkey used his trick again and fell into the water. But this time the trick was on him. The sponges became heavy with water and the weight ❸of his load greatly increased.❹

"I hope you've learned your lesson," the shopkeeper said to the donkey. "If you use a trick to avoid ❺ work, you will just end up with more work in the end."

**VOCABULARY**

1. **trick** n. ☞ たくらみ
2. **sponge** n. ☞ スポンジ
3. **weight** n. ☞ 重さ
4. **increase** v. ☞ 増える
5. **avoid** v. ☞ 避ける

*The Donkey and the Shopkeeper* **ロバと店主**

### 訳：ロバと店主

　働き者の店主が、市場に塩を買いにロバの手綱を引いていました。家への帰り道、小川を渡らなくてはいけませんでしたが、ロバはとても疲れていたので、岩の上で足を滑らせ、水に落ちてしまいました。
　ロバが驚いたのは、荷がひどく軽くなったことでした。水がほとんどの塩を流してしまっていたのです。店主はロバを市場に連れて戻り、今度はさらに多くの塩を買いました。小川にたどり着いたとき、今度は、ロバはわざと水に落ちました。

　店主はロバの悪知恵を見抜き、市場に戻って塩の代わりにスポンジを買いました。
　小川に着いたとき、ロバは再び悪知恵を働かせて水に落ちました。しかし、今度はロバが策略にはまる番でした。スポンジは水を吸って重くなり、荷の重さはひどく増してしまったのです。
「私は、お前に教訓を得てほしいんだよ」
店主はロバに言いました。
「仕事をさぼるためにごまかせば、結局もっと仕事をしなくてはいけなくなるんだよ」

【ことわざ】「楽あれば苦あり」

# The Bundle of Sticks
# 枝の束

An old farmer had two sons who fought[1] with each other all the time. The farmer often told them to stop fighting, but they never listened to him.

So one day, he asked his sons to bring him a bundle[2] of sticks.[3] "Can you break these sticks in half?" he asked his youngest son.

"Of course," said his youngest son. "Those sticks are thin.[4] I can break them like straw!"[5] He took the sticks from his father, but no matter how[6] hard he tried, he couldn't break them.

1. **fight** v.(fight-fought-fought) ☞ けんかする
2. **bundle** n. ☞ 束
3. **stick** n. ☞ 小枝
4. **thin** adj. ☞ 細い
5. **straw** n. ☞ わら
6. **no matter how** ☞ どんなに〜であろうとも

*The Bundle of Sticks* 枝の束 | 17

"Of course he failed," ❶ said the other son. "He is young and weak.❷ I will succeed❸ because I am the oldest and the strongest."❹

The oldest son then took the sticks, but he couldn't break them, either.

Then the father took out two sticks from the bundle and handed one to each son. "Can you break them now?" he asked. And of course they could.

"You can learn an important lesson❺ from these sticks," the farmer said to his sons. "Together, you are strong, but when you are alone, you can be broken easily."

**VOCABULARY**

1. **fail** v. ☞ 失敗する
2. **weak** adj. ☞ 弱い
3. **succeed** v. ☞ 成功する
4. **strong** adj. ☞ 強い
5. **lesson** n. ☞ 教訓

*The Bundle of Sticks* 枝の束

### 訳：枝の束

　年老いた農夫には、いつもケンカばかりしている2人の息子がいました。農夫は常々ケンカをやめるように言っていましたが、息子たちは聞く耳を持ちません。
　そこである日、農夫は息子たちに枝の束を持ってくるように言いました。
「これを半分に折れるかい？」
農夫は弟に聞きました。
　「もちろん」と弟は言いました。
「枝は細いから、わらみたいに折れますよ！」
父親から枝の束を取り上げましたが、どんなにがんばっても折ることはできません。

　「やっぱり失敗した」
もう1人の息子が言いました。
「弟は若くて弱い。僕は年上で力も強いから、できます」
　兄は束を取り上げますが、兄も枝を折ることはできません。
　すると父親は、束から2つの枝を抜き取り、2人の息子にそれぞれ1本ずつ渡しました。父は聞きます。
「今度は折れるかい？」
もちろん折ることができました。
　「お前たちはこの枝から大事な教訓を得られるはずだ」
農夫は息子たちに言いました。
「一緒になればお前たちは強い。しかし、1人1人のときは、簡単に折れてしまうものなのだ」

# The Fox and the Crow
# キツネとカラス

One day, a fox saw a crow ❶ sitting in a tree. The crow had a piece of cheese in her beak,❷ and she sat in the tree to eat it. The fox thought, "I want that cheese," and then he thought of a way to get it.

The fox walked to the foot of the tree and said, "Hello, Miss Crow. You look beautiful today."

"Really?" thought the crow while she looked down at the fox.

The fox said, "Your feathers ❸ are so colorful ❹ and your eyes are so bright.❺ But birds are not only beautiful to look at. They are also beautiful to listen to."

**VOCABULARY**

1. **crow** n. ☞ カラス
2. **beak** n. ☞ くちばし
3. **feather** n. ☞ 羽
4. **colorful** adj. ☞ 色鮮やかな
5. **bright** adj. ☞ 輝く

"Miss Crow, your voice is more beautiful than any other bird's," the fox said. "Please sing for me, and I will call you the Queen of Birds."

The crow smiled and lifted❶ her head. She began to sing, but when she opened her beak, the cheese dropped to the ground.

The fox quickly ate it. "Your voice is wonderful," he said, "but you are not very smart. You gave me your cheese, so I will give you some advice:❷ never trust❸ anyone who flatters❹ you."

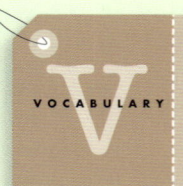

VOCABULARY

1. **lift** v. ☞ 持ち上げる
2. **advice** n. ☞ アドバイス
3. **trust** v. ☞ 信頼する
4. **flatter** v. ☞ お世辞を言う、こびへつらう

*The Fox and the Crow* **キツネとカラス**

## 訳：キツネとカラス

　ある日キツネは、木にとまっているカラスを見つけました。カラスは１切れのチーズをくわえ、それを食べようとしていました。
「あのチーズがほしいな」
そう思ったキツネは、奪う方法を考えました。
　キツネは木の根元まで歩いていき、言いました。
「こんにちは。カラスさん。今日はお美しいですね」
　「ホントかしら」
カラスはキツネを見下ろしながら考えました。
　キツネは言いました。
「カラスさんの羽はとても鮮やかで、目の色はとても明るい。でも鳥というものは、見て美しいだけではありません。聴いても美しいものです」

　「カラスさん。あなたの声は、ほかのどんな鳥より美しい」
キツネは言いました。
「僕のために歌ってください。そうしたらあなたのことを『鳥の女王』と呼びましょう」
　カラスは微笑み、頭をもたげて歌い出します。しかし、くちばしを開くと、チーズは地面に落ちてしまいました。
　キツネは急いでそれを食べました。そして言いました。
「カラスさんは、声は美しいけど、頭はあまりよくありませんね。僕にチーズをくれたから忠告をしましょう。お世辞を言う者は誰も信用してはいけません」

# The Emperor's New Clothes
# 裸の王様

There was once an emperor ❶ who thought only about clothes. Other emperors thought about building castles and larger kingdoms,❷ but this emperor thought only about clothes.

One day, two swindlers ❸ came to the emperor and said, "We have made a special cloth for you. It is special because only intelligent❹ people can see it."

"I must have a suit made from this special cloth," said the emperor. "Then I will be able to tell who is intelligent and who is not! Please make it for me at once!"

VOCABULARY

1. **emperor** n. ☞ 帝王
2. **kingdom** n. ☞ 王国
3. **swindler** n. ☞ 詐欺師
4. **intelligent** adj. ☞ 賢明な

*The Emperor's New Clothes* 裸の王様

When the emperor went to see the new suit, he saw nothing at all! "Oh, no!" he thought. "I am stupid!" The emperor was scared❶ and he pretended❷ to see the clothes.

The swindlers pretended to put the suit on him, and the emperor walked through the town. Everyone saw only underwear,❸ and they thought, "I am stupid!" So everyone pretended and shouted, "What beautiful clothes! What style!❹ What colors!"

Finally, a young boy said, "He isn't wearing anything at all!" And the emperor and all the people realized who was stupid. They all were.

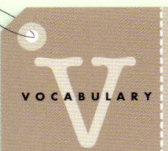

VOCABULARY

1. **scared** adj. ☞ 怖がる
2. **pretend** v. ☞ ふりをする
3. **underwear** n. ☞ 下着
4. **style** n. ☞ はやり、流行

*The Emperor's New Clothes* 裸の王様 | 31

### 訳：裸の王様

　昔、着るもののことしか考えない王様がいました。よその王様は城を建てることや、王国を拡大することを考えていましたが、この王様が考えるのは服のことだけ。
　ある日、2人の詐欺師が王様のところにやって来て言いました。
「王様のために特別な布を作りました。頭のよい人にしか見えない特別な布です」
　「その特別な布で服を作らないといけないな」
　と王様は言いました。
「そうすれば、誰が賢く、誰がそうでないのかがわかるぞ！すぐに作ってくれ！」

　王様が新しい服を見に行くと、王様には何も見えません！
「なんてことだ！」
　王様は思いました。
「私は愚か者だ！」
　怖くなった王様は、服が見えるふりをしました。
　詐欺師は王様に服を着せるふりをしました。そして、王様は町中を歩きました。人々に見えるのは下着だけです。人々は思いました。
「私は愚か者なんだ！」
　だから、みんなが見えるふりをして叫びました。
「なんて美しい服なんでしょう！流行の服ですね！なんて素敵な色でしょう！」
　ついに、1人の少年が言いました。
「何も着てないよ！」
　こうして王様と人々は誰が愚か者なのかを知ったのです。それは、自分たち全員でした。

# The Farmer's Treasure
# 農夫の宝物

There once was an old farmer. He was a hardworking man, so every year his harvest ❶ was very great.

One day, he became sick. He knew he would die soon. He wanted his two sons to look after the farm. "Long ago," he told them, "I put a great treasure ❷ in one of the vineyards."❸

After the farmer died, the sons began to dig ❹ carefully around the vines. ❺ Every day, they woke up early and worked until night. "We have to dig everywhere and find the treasure!" they said.

1. **harvest** n. ☞ 収穫高
2. **treasure** n. ☞ 宝
3. **vineyard** n. ☞ （ワイン用の）ブドウ園
4. **dig** v.(dig-dug-dug) ☞ 掘る
5. **vine** n. ☞ ブドウの木

The two sons dug all summer, but they didn't find the treasure. They were tired and sad. They sat down near the fields ❶ and talked one day.

"Maybe our father was only dreaming," ❷ said the older son. The younger son was looking at the vineyards. The vines were full of big, juicy ❸ grapes. Suddenly, he understood. "Brother, this great harvest is our treasure!"

The older brother looked at the vines. "You're right! Our father has taught us a wonderful lesson: Hard work brings great rewards." ❹

**VOCABULARY**

1. **field** n. ☞ 畑
2. **dream** v. ☞ 夢を見る
3. **juicy** adj. ☞ みずみずしい
4. **reward** n. ☞ ほうび

*The Farmer's Treasure* **農夫の宝物**

**訳：農夫の宝物**

　かつて1人の老いた農夫がいました。彼は働き者だったので、毎年たくさんの収穫がありました。

　しかしある日、病気になってしまいます。農夫は自分がもう長くはないことを知っていました。農夫は2人の息子に農園の世話をしてほしいと思っていました。彼は息子たちに言いました。
「昔、私はブドウ畑のひとつにたいそうな宝を埋めた」
　農夫が死んだ後、息子たちはブドウの木のまわりを注意深く掘り始めました。毎日、彼らは朝早く起き、夜まで働きました。
「あらゆるところを掘って、宝物を見つけなくちゃ！」
と息子たちは言いました。

　2人の息子は夏の間中ずっと掘りましたが、宝物を見つけることはありませんでした。彼らは疲れ、悲しい気持ちになりました。ある日、2人は畑の近くに腰を下ろし、話しました。
「たぶん、お父さんは夢を見ていただけなんだ」と兄が言いました。弟はブドウ畑を見ていました。ブドウの木には、大きく、水分をたっぷり含んだブドウがたわわに実っていました。突然、弟は理解したのです。
「お兄さん、この素晴らしい収穫物こそ僕たちの宝物だ！」
　兄はブドウの木を見ました。
「お前の言う通りだ！お父さんは僕たちに素晴らしい教訓を与えてくれたんだ。一生懸命働けば、素晴らしい報酬がある、と」

# The Eagle and the Farmer
# ワシと農夫

*The Eagle and the Farmer* **ワシと農夫** | 39

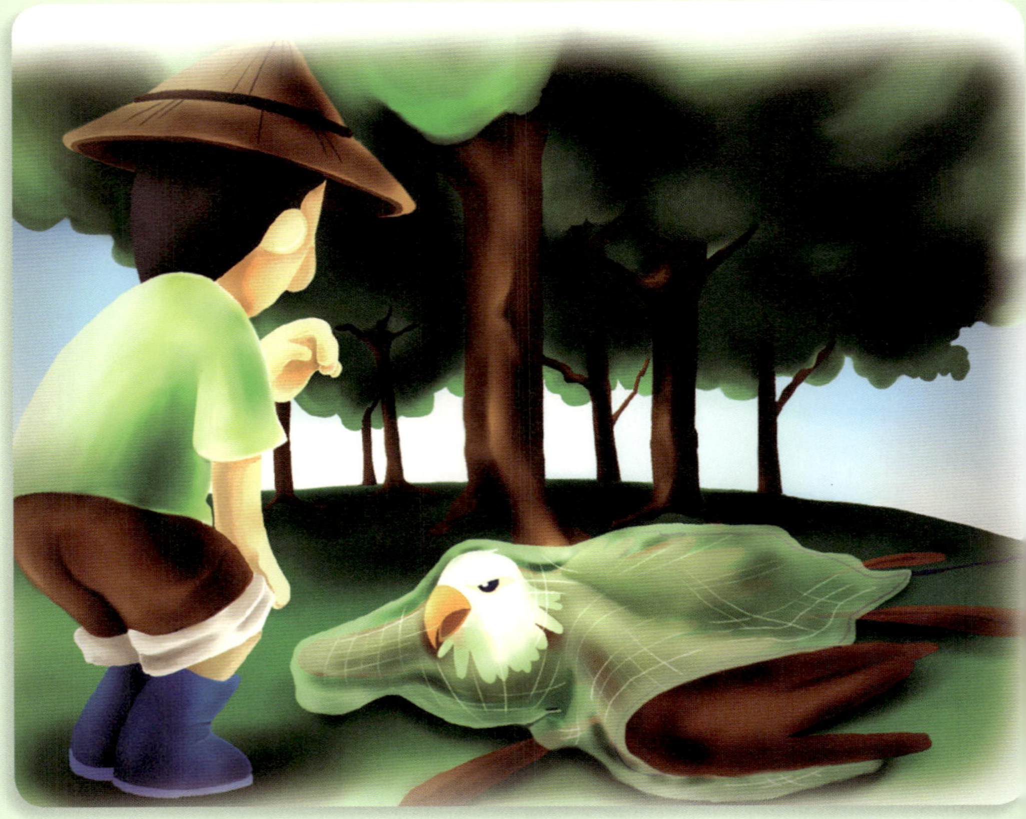

One beautiful summer morning, a farmer went to check his animal traps.❶ In one trap, he found a beautiful eagle. At first, he thought that he would kill the eagle and eat it.

But then he thought to himself, "This is a beautiful and special bird. It often catches rabbits and mice that eat my crops.❷ I'll let it go."

He opened the trap, and the eagle spread❸ its wings and flew up into the blue sky.

The eagle was very grateful❹ to be free again. It continued to live on the farmer's land and catch mice and rabbits.

**VOCABULARY**

1. **trap** n. ☞ わな
2. **crop** n. ☞ 農作物
3. **spread** v. (spread-spread-spread) ☞ 広げる
4. **grateful** adj. ☞ 感謝する

*The Eagle and the Farmer* **ワシと農夫**

CD.12·13

Later that summer, the farmer was building a wall. It was high and made of large stones.❶ Suddenly, the wall started to fall, but the farmer did not notice.

The eagle, flying above, saw that the farmer was in danger. It flew down and grabbed❷ the farmer's hat off his head. The farmer shouted, "Hey! Bring that back!"

The eagle flew a short distance❸ and then dropped the hat. The angry farmer picked up his hat and walked back. He saw that the stone wall had fallen. The farmer smiled and thought, "The eagle repaid❹ me when I most needed help."

**VOCABULARY**

1. **stone** n. ☞ 石
2. **grab** v. ☞ ひっつかむ、つかみ取る
3. **distance** n. ☞ 距離
4. **repay** v.(repay-repaid-repaid) ☞ 〜に報いる

*The Eagle and the Farmer* **ワシと農夫** | 43

### 訳：ワシと農夫

　ある晴れた朝、農夫は動物にしかけた罠を調べに行くと、ひとつの罠に美しいワシがかかっていました。はじめはワシを殺して食べてしまおうと思いました。
　でも、農夫はひそかに考えました。
「これは美しく特別な鳥だ。私の作物を食べるウサギやネズミをよく捕まえてくれる。放してやろう」
　農夫が罠をはずすと、ワシは羽を広げ、青い空に飛び立っていきました。
　ワシは再び自由の身になれたことにとても感謝しました。農夫の土地で暮らし、ネズミやウサギを獲り続けました。

　その夏、農夫は壁を作っていました。それは背の高いもので、大きな石でできていました。突然、その壁が倒れ始めますが、農夫は気づきません。
　上空を飛んでいたワシが、農夫に危険が迫っていることに気づきました。ワシは舞い降りると農夫の帽子をつかみました。農夫は叫びました。
「おい！　帽子を返せ！」
　ワシは少し離れた場所まで飛ぶと帽子を落としました。怒った農夫は帽子を拾うと歩いて戻りました。そして石の壁が倒れているのを見つけるのです。農夫は微笑み、思いました。
「ワシは、私がもっとも助けを必要としているときに恩返しをしてくれたんだな」

【ことわざ】「情けは人の為ならず」

# 農夫とロバ

*The Farmer and the Donkey*

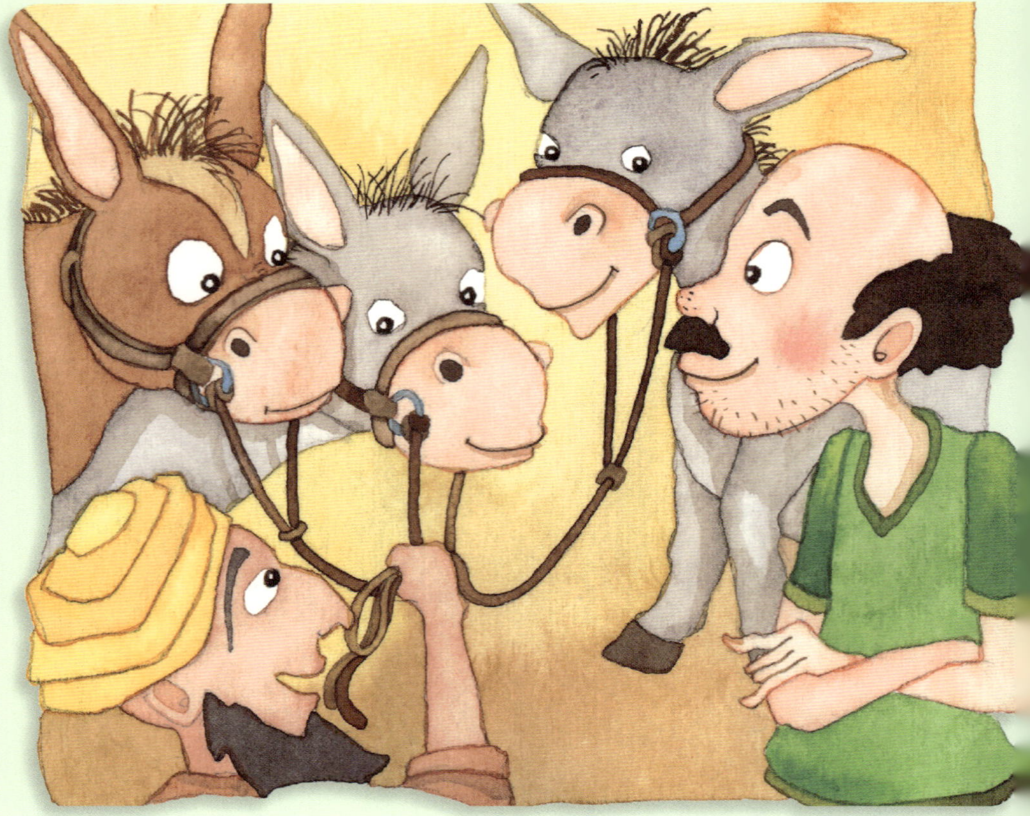

There once was a farmer who wanted to buy a donkey. He wanted a hardworking one that could help him on his farm. He went to a market and saw one that looked perfect.❶

"May I try out this donkey for a day or two?" asked the farmer. "If he is hardworking, I will pay❷ you a good price."❸

"Of course you may," said the seller. ❹ "I'm sure that he will please you." The farmer thanked the seller and took the donkey back to his farm.

---

**VOCABULARY**

1. **perfect** adj. ☞ 申し分がない
2. **pay** v. (pay-paid-paid) ☞ 支払う
3. **price** n. ☞ 値段
4. **seller** n. ☞ 売主

*The Farmer and the Donkey* **農夫とロバ**

When they arrived,❶ the new donkey joined❷ the other animals on the farm. He placed ❸himself beside❹ the fattest, laziest donkeys there. The farmer shook his head and took him back to the seller.

"Show me another donkey," said the farmer. "I don't want this one." He told the seller about what the donkey had done.

"I don't understand," said the seller. "What's wrong with standing beside lazy donkeys?"

"Well," said the farmer, "you can understand a lot about someone if you look at the friends he chooses."

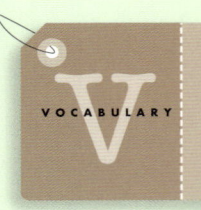

VOCABULARY

1. **arrive** v. ☞ 着く
2. **join** v. ☞ 〜に加わる
3. **place** v. ☞ 〜を置く
4. **beside** prep. ☞ 〜のそばに

*The Farmer and the Donkey* 農夫とロバ | 49

The Farmer and the Donkey

### 訳：農夫とロバ

　昔々、ロバを買いたい農夫がいました。自分の農場で力になってくれる働き者のロバがほしかったのです。農夫は市場に行って、おあつらえ向きに見えるロバを見つけました。
「1日か2日、このロバを試しに使ってみてもいいかね」
農夫は聞きました。
「もしよく働いたら、高く買うよ」
　「もちろんいいですよ」と売り主は言いました。
「きっと満足いただけると思います」
農夫は売り主に礼を言い、農場にロバを連れて帰りました。

　到着すると、新しいロバは農場にいるほかの動物たちに加わりました。ロバは、そこで最も太った怠け者のロバたちのそばに陣取りました。農夫は頭を左右に振り、ロバを売り主に戻しました。
　「別のロバを見せてくれ」と農夫は言いました。
「これは要らない」
農夫は売り主に、そのロバが何をしたかを話しました。
　売り主は言いました。
「わかりません。怠け者のロバたちのそばに立って何が悪いんですか」
　農夫は言いました。
「いいかい。選ぶ友人を見れば、その人物のことがよくわかるはずだ」

**【ことわざ】**「類は友を呼ぶ」

# The Wind and the Sun
# 北風と太陽

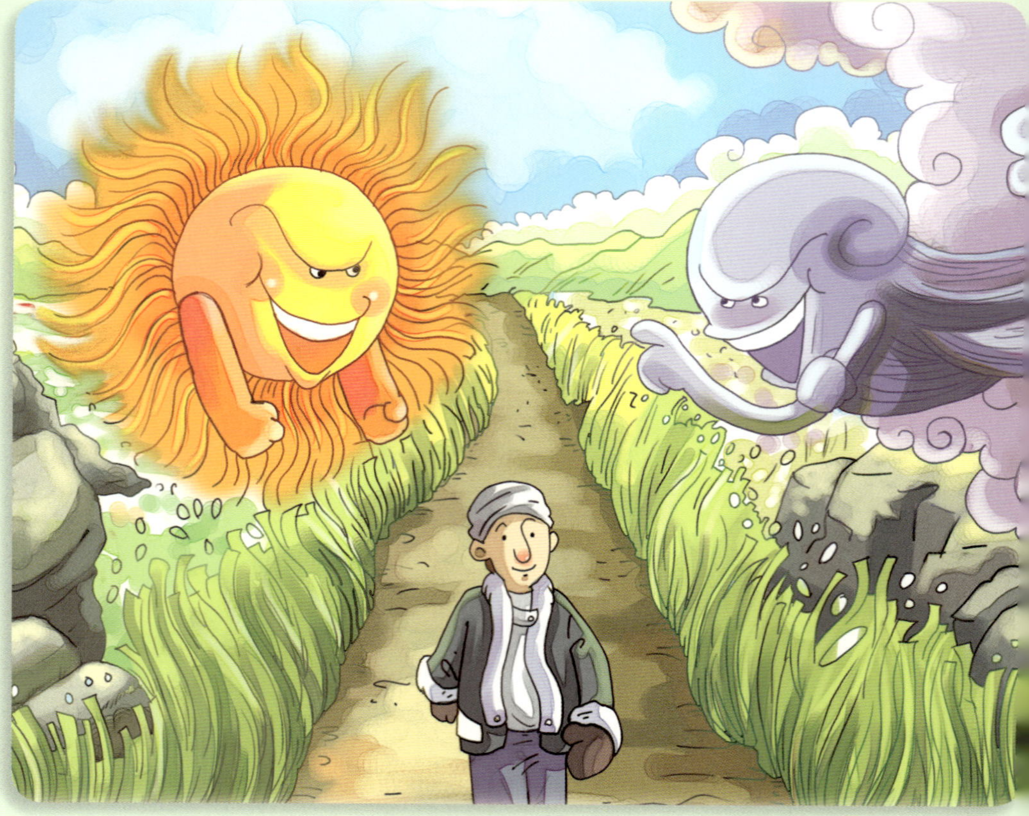

One day, the wind and the sun were arguing about who was the strongest. "It is clear that I am the strongest," said the wind. "When I blow, branches ❶break off the trees, and the waves ❷beat ❸on the shore."❹

"That's nothing," said the sun. "I am much stronger than that." Just then, they saw a man wearing a heavy coat. "We will both try to make this man take off his coat," said the sun. "Whoever succeeds will be the strongest."

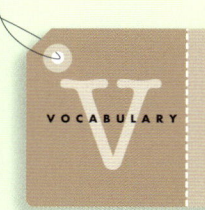

**VOCABULARY**

1. **branch** n. ☞ 枝
2. **wave** n. ☞ 波
3. **beat** v.(beat-beat-beaten) ☞ 打つ
4. **shore** n. ☞ 海岸

*The Wind and the Sun* 北風と太陽

The wind agreed to go first. He blew hard at the man, but it was no use. ❶ The man became cold and held onto ❷ his coat with both hands.

Then it was the sun's turn. ❸ He came out from behind a cloud and shone gently ❹ down on the man. The man smiled and took off his coat to enjoy ❺ the warm sunshine.

"You see?" asked the sun. "Kindness and gentleness are stronger than anything in the world."

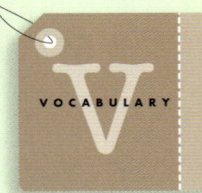

**VOCABULARY**

1. **no use** ☞ 全く役に立たない
2. **hold onto** v. ☞ 〜をしっかりつかまえておく
3. **turn** n. ☞ 順番
4. **gently** adv. ☞ 優しく
5. **enjoy** v. ☞ 楽しむ

*The Wind and the Sun* 北風と太陽 | 55

### 訳：北風と太陽

　ある日、風と太陽が、誰が最強か議論していました。
「おれが最強なのは明らかさ」
と風が言いました。
「おれが吹けば、枝は木々から折れて落ち、波は岸辺に打ちつける」
　「話にならないな」
と太陽は言いました。
「そんなのより僕のほうがずっと強い」
　ちょうどそのとき、2人は厚いコートを着た1人の男を見つけました。
「この男のコートを脱がせてみよう」
と太陽が言いました。
「成功したほうが最強だ」

　風は先に挑戦することを承知しました。風は男に向かって強く吹きつけましたが、まったく役に立ちません。男は寒くなって両手でコートをしっかりつかんだからです。
　次は太陽の番です。太陽は雲の陰から姿を現し、やさしく男を照らしました。男は微笑み、暖かい陽の光を満喫するためにコートを脱ぎました。
　「わかった？」
と太陽は聞きました。
　「世界では親切とやさしさは何ものにも増して強いのさ」

# The Fox and the Goat
# キツネとヤギ

58

One day, a fox fell into ❶ a deep well ❷ and could not get out. A thirsty ❸ goat looked down into the well. He saw the fox. "How is the water?" asked the goat.

"The water is cool and delicious," said the clever fox. "Come in and have a drink!" The goat was terribly ❹ thirsty. He jumped into the well without giving it a second thought. ❺ "But how will I get out?" asked the goat.

**VOCABULARY**

1. **fall into** v. ☞ 〜に落ちる
2. **well** n. ☞ 井戸
3. **thirsty** adj. ☞ のどの渇いた
4. **terribly** adv. ☞ ものすごく
5. **give ~ a second thought** v. ☞ 〜について考え直す

*The Fox and the Goat* **キツネとヤギ**

"We'll help each other," said the fox. "Put your front feet on the wall. I will climb up your back. Then I will help you get out."

The goat agreed. He placed his feet on the wall. The fox quickly climbed out and started to run away.❶ "Come back!" cried the goat. "I can't get out of the well by myself!"

The fox turned back and said, "You silly old goat! Jumping into the well was a foolish❷ decision.❸ You should always think twice before you act."❹

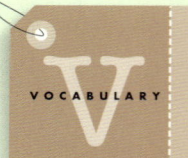

**VOCABULARY**
1. **run away** v. ☞ 走り去る
2. **foolish** adj. ☞ おろかな
3. **decision** n. ☞ 決断
4. **act** v. ☞ 行動する

*The Fox and the Goat* **キツネとヤギ**

## 訳：キツネとヤギ

　ある日、1匹のキツネが深い井戸に落ち、出られなくなってしまいました。のどの渇いたヤギが井戸をのぞき込むと、キツネがいます。
「水はどんな感じ?」
ヤギは聞きました。
　「冷たくておいしいよ」
ずる賢いキツネは言いました。
「ここに来て飲んでみなよ!」
　とてものどが渇いていたヤギは、考え直しもせずに井戸に飛び込みました。
「でも、どうやって出るの?」
ヤギは聞きました。

　「助け合うんだよ」とキツネは言います。
「前足を壁につけてみて。僕が君の背中を登って行く。それから僕が君の脱出を手助けする」
　ヤギは承知して、足を壁につけました。しかしキツネは素早く登ると、逃げ出しました。
「帰ってきてくれよ!」
ヤギは叫びます。
「僕だけじゃ井戸から出られないよ!」
　キツネは引き返してきて言いました。
「間抜けな老いぼれヤギさん!　井戸に飛び込むなんて馬鹿げてる。いつも行動に移す前にもう1度よく考えるべきなんだ」

# The Donkey and the Horse
# ロバとウマ

64

A farmer wanted to bring ten bags of rice to the market and sell them. He put five bags of rice on his horse and five bags of rice on his donkey.

The bags were very heavy,❶ and soon❷ the donkey became tired. "Please," he said to the horse, "could you carry one of my bags for me? They're so heavy, and you are stronger than I am."

"No," said the horse. "I serve❸ the farmer, not you. He gave me five bags to carry, not six! You must do your job, and I must do mine."

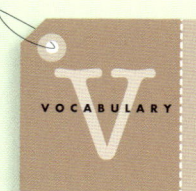

---

**VOCABULARY**

1. **heavy** adj. ☞ 重い
2. **soon** adv. ☞ 間もなく
3. **serve** v. ☞ ～に仕える

The farmer, the horse, and the donkey continued walking under the hot sun. The poor donkey became more and more tired. Suddenly,❶ he fell over at the side of the road.

The farmer tried to pull the donkey to its feet, but the donkey was too tired to move. Then the farmer took the donkey's five bags of rice and put them on the horse.

The horse realized ❷ he had made a big mistake. ❸ "If I had agreed to help the donkey," he cried, "I'd only have to carry one extra❹ bag. Now I must carry all ten!"

---

**VOCABULARY**

1. **suddenly** adv. ☞ 突然に
2. **realize** v. ☞ 悟る
3. **mistake** n. ☞ 過ち、間違い
4. **extra** adj. ☞ 余分な

*The Donkey and the Horse* **ロバとウマ**

The Donkey and the Horse

### 訳:ロバとウマ

　農夫は、10袋の米を市場に持っていき、売りたいと考えました。農夫は、米5袋をウマに、5袋をロバに載せました。
　袋はとても重く、ロバはすぐに疲れてしまいました。
「お願いだ」とロバはウマに言いました。
「僕の袋をひとつ運んでくれないか？　とても重いんだ。君は僕より強いから」
「いやだね」
　ウマは言いました。
「僕は農夫に仕えているんだ。君にじゃない。彼は僕が運ぶ分として5袋与えた。6袋じゃない。君は君の仕事、僕は僕の仕事をすべきだ」

　農夫とウマとロバは照りつける太陽のもと、歩き続けました。かわいそうなロバはどんどん疲れていきます。そして突然、道端に倒れてしまいました。農夫はロバを引っ張り起こそうとしましたが、ロバは疲れ果てて動くことができません。すると農夫は、ロバの5つの米袋を取りはずすと、ウマに載せました。
　ウマは大きな間違いをしていたことに気付き、泣きました。
「もし僕がロバを助けることを聞き入れていたら、ひとつだけ余計に運ぶだけですんだのに。今は10袋すべて運ばなくちゃいけない！」

【ことわざ】「後悔先に立たず」

# The Travelers and the Bear
# 旅人とクマ

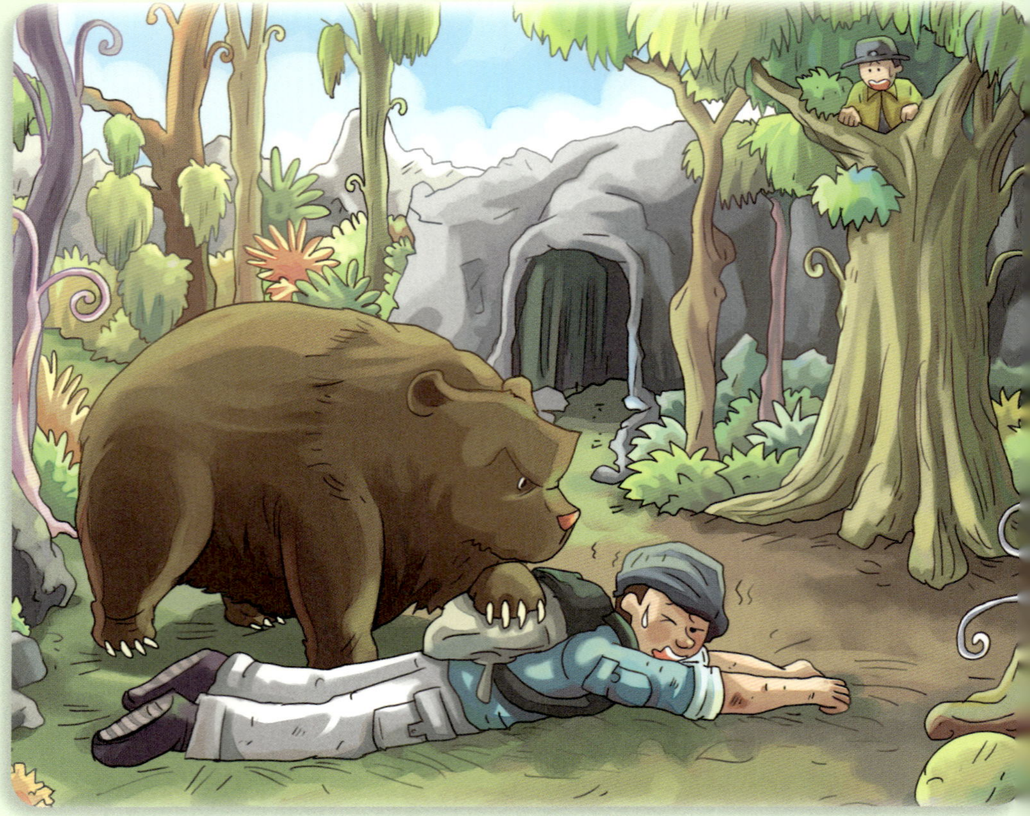

Once upon a time,[1] two friends were traveling[2] together in a forest. Suddenly, a bear jumped out onto the path.[3]

One friend saw the bear first. He quickly climbed up a tree and hid. He did not stop to help his friend.

The other friend was left alone with the bear. He had to think fast. The bear moved closer to the man.

The man fell down to the ground and did not move. The bear came up to the man and began to smell[4] him.

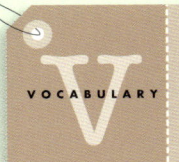

**VOCABULARY**

1. **once upon a time** ☞ 昔々のこと
2. **travel** v. ☞ 旅する
3. **path** n. ☞ 小道
4. **smell** v. ☞ においを嗅ぐ

*The Travelers and the Bear* **旅人とクマ**

The man held his breath and lay perfectly still.❶ Soon, the bear lost interest in the man and left. When it was clear❷ that the bear was gone, the man in the tree came down to the ground.

He was very happy to see that his friend was safe. "That bear was so close that it looked like it was talking to you!" he joked.❸ "What did it say?"

"The bear gave me this advice," said the man. "Never travel with a friend who deserts❹ you when there is trouble."❺

**VOCABULARY**
1. **still** adj. ☞ じっとした、動かない
2. **clear** adj. ☞ はっきりとわかった
3. **joke** v. ☞ 冗談を言う
4. **desert** v. ☞ 〜を見捨てる
5. **trouble** n. ☞ トラブル

*The Travelers and the Bear* 旅人とクマ

**訳：旅人とクマ**

　昔々、友人同士の2人が森を旅していました。すると突然、クマが小道に飛び出してきました。
　1人は先にクマを見つけ、素早く木に登り、姿を隠しました。彼は友人を助けようと立ち止まったりしませんでした。
　もう1人はクマとともに残されてしまいました。素早く頭を働かせなくてはいけません。クマは迫ってきます。
　男は地面に倒れ、じっとしていました。クマは男に近づき、匂いをかぎはじめました。

　男は息を止め、ぴくりともしません。間もなくクマは男に興味を失い、去ってしまいました。クマが完全に姿を消したとき、木に隠れていた男が地面に降りてきました。
　男は、友人が無事だったのがわかり、とても喜びました。
「クマがあまりにも近づくから、君に話しかけているように見えたよ」
と冗談を言いました。
「クマは何て言ってたんだい？」
　「クマは僕に忠告してくれたよ」
と男は言いました。
「何かトラブルが起きたとき、君を見捨てるような友人とは旅行するな、ってね」

# The Mosquito and the Lion
# 蚊とライオン

A mosquito ❶ went up to a lion and said, "Everyone says you are the strongest animal in the world."

"That's right," said the lion. "I am big and strong, and I have sharp teeth."

"Well, I'm not afraid of you," said the mosquito. "I am going to fight you, and I am going to win!"

"You could never win," laughed ❷ the lion. "I am a thousand times stronger than you."

"Here I come!" cried the mosquito, and he flew toward ❸ the lion's face.

**VOCABULARY**

1. **mosquito** n. ☞ 蚊
2. **laugh** v. ☞ 笑う
3. **toward** prep. ☞ 〜に向かって

The Mosquito and the Lion **蚊とライオン**

The mosquito landed ❶ on the lion's nose and bit him again and again. The lion tried to sink his teeth into the mosquito, but the mosquito was too small.

"I give up!" said the lion. "Please don't bite me anymore."

"I won!" shouted the mosquito as he flew away. But he didn't look where he was going, and he became trapped in a spider's web. ❷

"How strange," thought the mosquito. "I defeated ❸ a lion, but a tiny ❹ spider can defeat me."

**VOCABULARY**

1. **land** v. ☞ 着地する
2. **web** n. ☞ クモの巣
3. **defeat** v. ☞ 負かす
4. **tiny** adj. ☞ とても小さい

*The Mosquito and the Lion* **蚊とライオン**

### 訳：蚊とライオン

　1匹の蚊がライオンによじ上って言いました。
「みんな、あなたが世界でいちばん強い動物だと言っていますよ」
　「その通りだ」
ライオンは言いました。
「おれさまは大きくて強い。そして鋭い歯を持っている」
　「でも、僕はあなたがこわくありません」と蚊は言いました。
「あなたと戦って倒すことができますよ！」
　「お前が勝てるわけがない」とライオンは笑いました。
「おれはお前の1000倍も強い」
　「じゃあ、行きますよ！」
蚊は大声を上げると、ライオンの顔に向かって飛びました。

　蚊はライオンの鼻の上に止まると、何度も刺しました。ライオンは、歯で蚊をかもうとしますが、蚊は小さすぎました。
　「降参だ！」とライオンは言いました。
「もう刺さないでくれ」
　「勝った！」
蚊は飛び去りながら叫びました。しかし、前を見ていなかった蚊はクモの巣にひっかかってしまいました。
　「おかしいな」
蚊は考えました。
「僕はライオンを倒したのに、小さなクモに負かされてしまった」

# The Thirsty Crow
# のどの渇いたカラス

82

There once lived a young crow in the countryside. One summer, there was no rain, and it was very hot. The crow was very thirsty, but he couldn't find any water.

"How can I survive?"❶ he thought. "I must have water or I'll die!" Just then he saw a farmhouse. Outside❷ the house, there was a vase❸ with some water at the bottom.❹ He tried to drink, but he couldn't reach the water inside.

The young crow didn't know what to do. He leaned against the vase and cried.

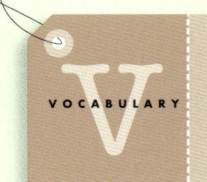

---

**VOCABULARY**

1. **survive** v. ☞ 生き延びる
2. **outside** prep. ☞ ～の外で
3. **vase** n. ☞ 花瓶
4. **bottom** n. ☞ 底

*The Thirsty Crow* **のどの渇いたカラス**

"Will somebody please help me?" sobbed ❶ the crow. He cried and cried, but nobody heard him. Finally, he dried ❷ his eyes and stood up.

He tried knocking over the vase, but it was too heavy. Then he tried breaking it, but he wasn't strong enough. Finally, he had a good idea. He began dropping stones into the vase. The water slowly rose to the top. At last, the crow could drink.

"What wonderful water!" said the crow. "I'm glad ❸ that I didn't waste ❹ all my time by crying. Thinking is much better than crying!"

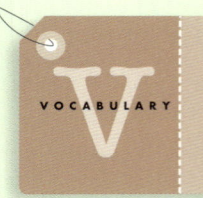

**VOCABULARY**

1. **sob** v. ☞ すすり泣く
2. **dry** v. ☞ 〜を乾かす
3. **glad** adj. ☞ 嬉しく思う
4. **waste** v. ☞ むだにする

*The Thirsty Crow* **のどの渇いたカラス** | 85

### 訳:のどの渇いたカラス

　昔、田舎に1羽の若いカラスがいました。ある年、雨がまったく降らず、とても暑い夏がありました。カラスはとてものどが渇いていましたが、水が見つかりません。
「どうやって生き伸びたらいいんだ」
とカラスは思いました。
「水がなければ死んでしまう！」
　ちょうどそのとき、農家が見えました。家の外に、底にいくらかの水が残された花瓶がありました。カラスは飲もうとしましたが、中の水に届きません。
　若いカラスはどうしたらいいかわかりません。花瓶に寄りかかって泣きました。

　「誰か僕を助けて」
　カラスはすすり泣きました。泣き続けましたが、誰もその声を聞きつけてはくれません。カラスはようやく涙を拭くと、立ち上がりました。
　花瓶をひっくり返そうとしましたが、重すぎました。今度は壊そうとしましたが、そこまで力がありませんでした。ついに、いいアイデアを思いつき、花瓶の中に石を落とし始めました。水はゆっくりと口のほうに上がっていきます。ついにカラスは飲むことができたのです。
「なんて素晴らしい水なんだ！」
　カラスは言いました。
「嘆いて時間を無駄にしなくてよかった。嘆くより考えるほうがずっといい」

# The Old Dog
# 老犬

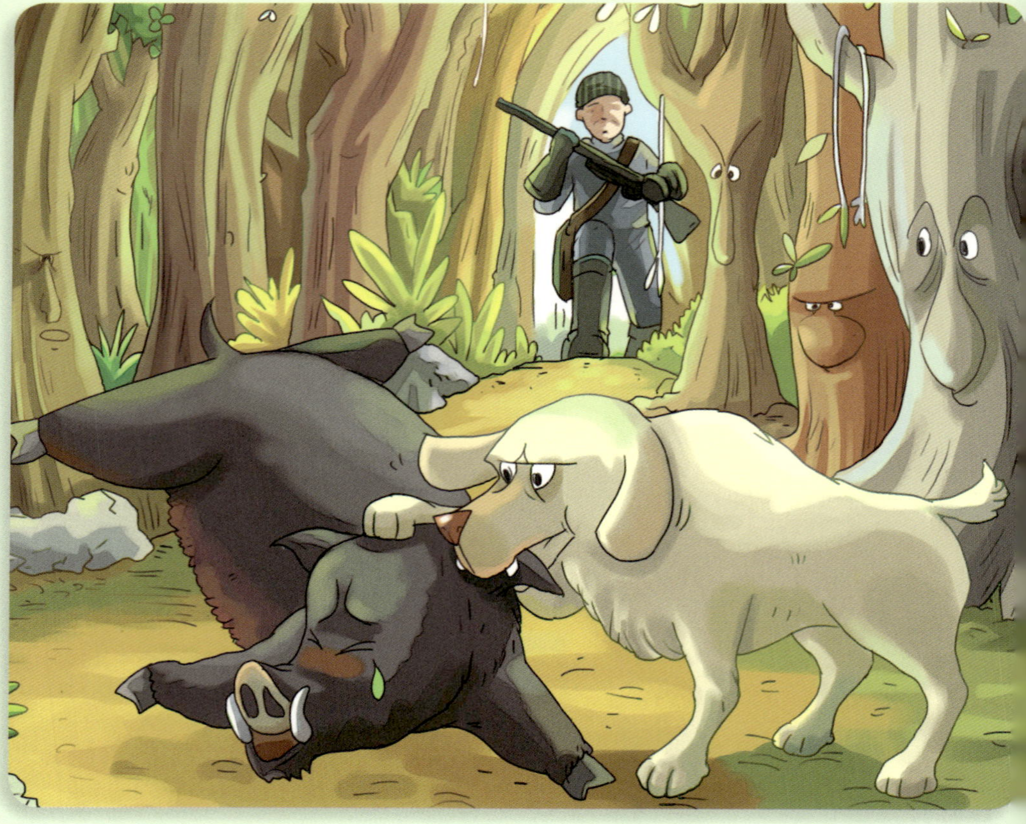

There once lived an old dog. When he was young, he was a great hunter and his master ❶ loved him very much. Now, though, he was becoming slow and weak.

One day, the old dog and his master were walking in the forest. The dog saw a pig and chased ❷ it. He caught ❸ the pig by its ear, but his teeth were weak, and the pig got away.

"My teeth were much stronger when I was young," thought the dog. "I hope my master isn't mad." ❹

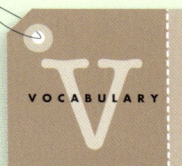

**VOCABULARY**

1. **master** n. ☞ 主人
2. **chase** v. ☞ 追いかける
3. **catch** v.(catch-caught-caught) ☞ 捕まえる
4. **mad** adj. ☞ 怒って

*The Old Dog* **老犬**

When the master saw the pig run away, he was angry. ❶ "You useless dog!" he shouted. "What will my family eat tonight?"

The dog was sad. "Master," he said, "it is not my fault ❷ that I'm old. For many years, I've helped you to feed your family. Am I worth nothing to you now?"

The master realized that he was wrong. "You're right," he said. "I shouldn't blame you for being old. I should praise ❸ you for all your years of service." ❹

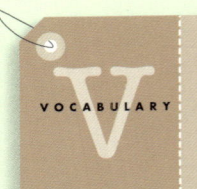

**VOCABULARY**

1. **angry** adj. ☞ 怒って
2. **fault** n. ☞ 過ち
3. **praise** v. ☞ 〜をほめる
4. **service** n. ☞ 奉仕

The Old Dog 老犬 | 91

## The Old Dog

**訳：老犬**

　昔々、1匹の老犬が暮らしていました。若いときは立派なハンターで、主人は犬をたいそうかわいがりました。しかし今は、だんだん動きはのろくなり、体は弱ってきていました。

　ある日、老犬とその主人は森を歩いていました。犬はブタを見つけ、追いかけました。犬は、ブタの耳をかんで捕まえましたが、歯が弱かったため、ブタは逃げてしまいました。
「若い頃は私の歯もずっと強かった」
と犬は思いました。
「ご主人様が怒っていないといいが」

　主人はブタが逃げたのを見ると怒りました。
「役立たずの犬め！」
　主人は大声を上げました。
「私の家族は今夜、何を食べればいいんだ？」
　犬は悲しくなりました。
「ご主人様」と犬は言いました。
「年老いたのは、私の過ちではありません。長年、私はあなたの家族を養う手伝いをしてきました。もう私には何の価値もないのでしょうか」
　主人は、自分が間違っていたことに気づきました。
「お前の言う通りだ」
　主人は言いました。
「年老いたことを責めるべきではないのだ。長年仕えてくれたことをたたえるべきなのだ」

# The Old Woman and the Doctor
# おばあさんと医者

An old woman lost her sight ❶ and called a doctor for help. She said, "If you heal ❷ me, I will give you a large sum ❸ of money." And she said this in front of many people.

The doctor agreed, and he came every day to put medicine in her eyes. But each time he came, he stole something from her house.

Finally, he stole all of her valuable things. Then he gave her new medicine and healed her. When he was done, he demanded ❹ that she give him the money.

But the woman saw that her things were gone, and said no.

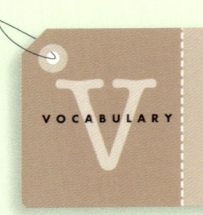

1. **sight** n. ☞ 視力
2. **heal** v. ☞ 治す
3. **sum** n. ☞ 金額
4. **demand** v. ☞ 要求する

*The Old Woman and the Doctor* **おばあさんと医者** | 95

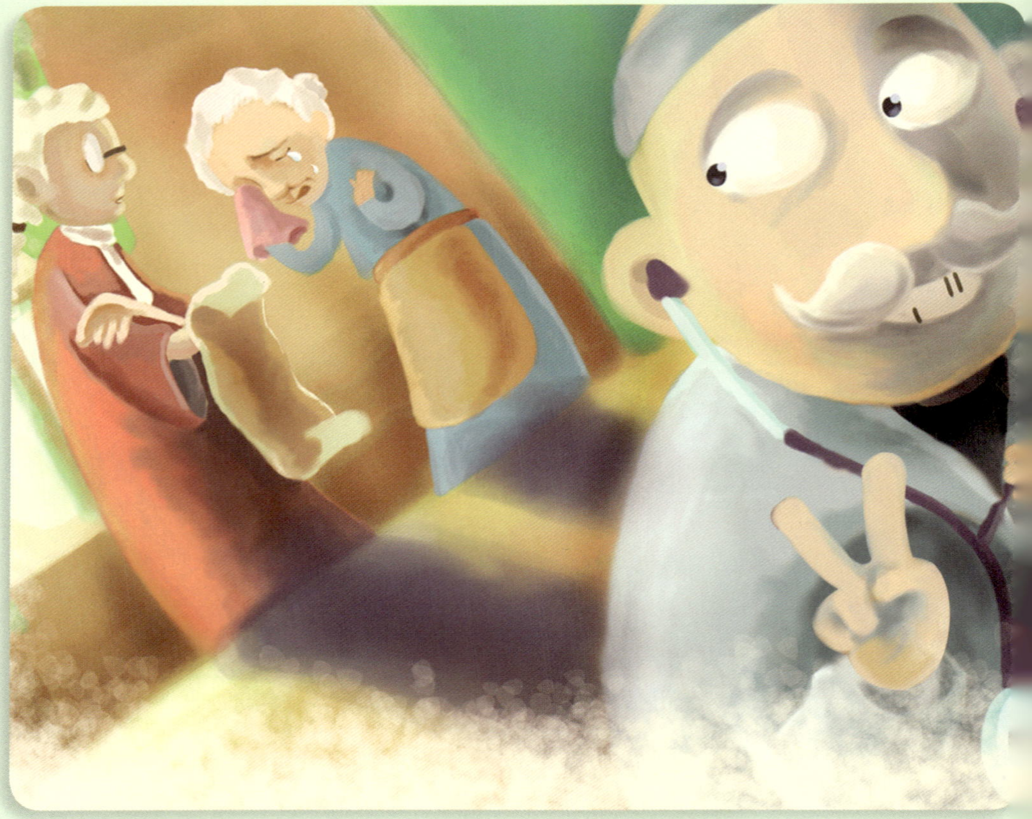

The doctor brought a judge ❶ to the woman's house. He thought, "I will certainly ❷ win such a simple case."❸

The judge asked the woman, "Did you promise ❹ to give him money?" The doctor said, "She did. Many people heard."

The woman said sadly, "It is true," and the doctor smiled.

But then she said, "Before I lost my sight, though, I saw valuable things in my house. Many people also saw them, but now I don't see them. So the doctor has not really healed my eyes."

The judge decided that the woman was right.

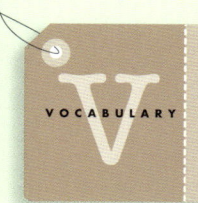

---

**VOCABULARY**

1. **judge** n. ☞ 裁判官
2. **certainly** adv. ☞ 確実に
3. **case** n. ☞ 事例、案件
4. **promise** v. ☞ 約束する

*The Old Woman and the Doctor* **おばあさんと医者**

### 訳：おばあさんと医者

　1人のおばあさんは、目が見えなくなってしまい、医者に助けを求めました。おばあさんは言いました。
「もし私を治してくれたら、大金をあげましょう」
　おばあさんはこのことをたくさんの人の前で言いました。
　医者は承諾しました。そして毎日やって来て、おばあさんの目に薬をつけました。しかし、医者は来る度に、おばあさんの家から何かしら盗んでいきます。
　ついに医者はおばあさんの貴重な品々をすべて盗みました。そして医者はおばあさんに新しい薬を与え、治したのです。医者は事を成し遂げると、おばあさんに金をくれと要求しました。
　しかし、おばあさんは、自分の持ち物がなくなっていることを知り、断ります。

　医者は、おばあさんの家に裁判官を連れていきました。医者は思いました。
「こんな単純な案件だ。絶対に僕が勝つ」
　裁判官はおばあさんにたずねました。
「あなたは、彼にお金を与えると約束したのですか」
　医者が言いました。
「そう言ったんです。多くの人が聞いています」
おばあさんが「それは本当です」と悲しそうに言うと、医者は笑みを浮かべました。
　しかしその後、おばあさんは言ったのです。
「でも、私が視力を失う前には、私の家の貴重品が見えていました。それはたくさんの人たちも見ています。でも今、私には何も見えません。だから、お医者さんは私の目を本当に治したわけではないのです」
　裁判官は、おばあさんが正しいと判決を下しました。

# The Proud Heron
# 高慢なサギ

The Proud Heron **高慢なサギ** | 99

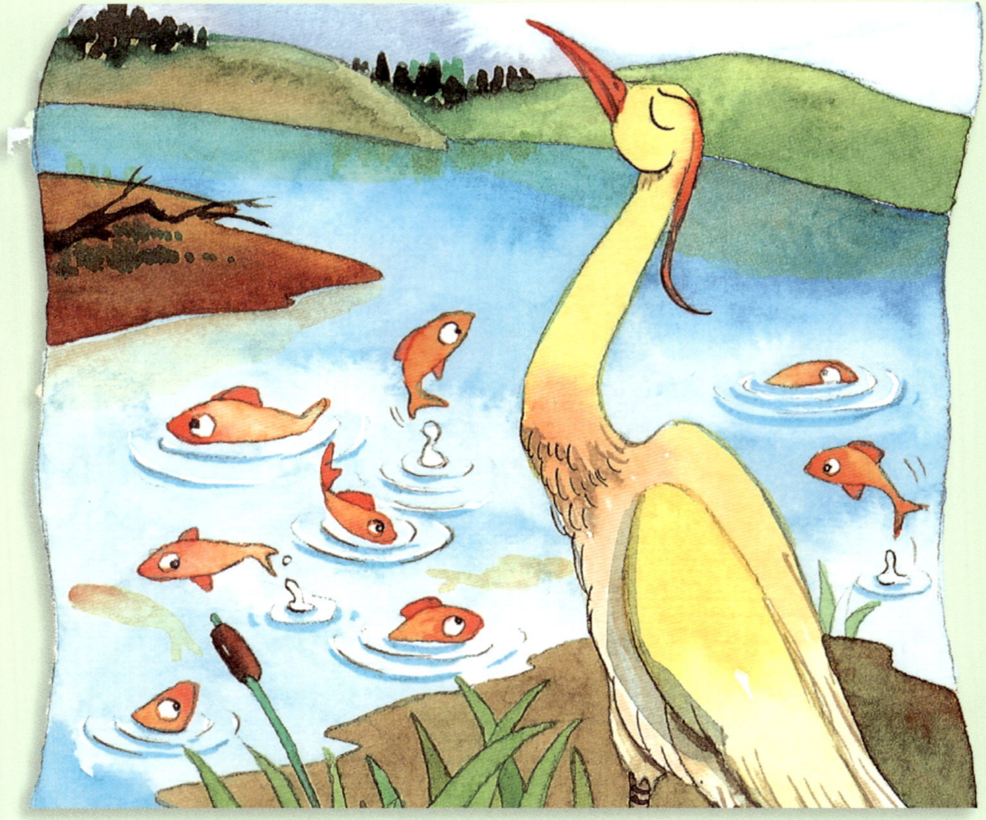

There once was a proud heron.① She thought she was the wisest and most beautiful heron in the world.

One morning, she stood beside a stream② and looked into the water. She wanted to have a big, fat fish for breakfast. "There are a lot of fish here," she said, "but they're too small for me. I deserve③ only the biggest and the best!"

Just then, a bigger fish swam near the shore, but the heron still wasn't interested.④ "I wouldn't bother⑤ to open my mouth for such a small fish!" she said.

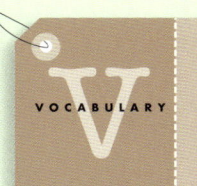

**VOCABULARY**

1. **heron** n. ☞ サギ
2. **stream** n. ☞ 小川
3. **deserve** v. ☞ ～を受けるに値する
4. **interested** adj. ☞ 興味があって、関心がある
5. **bother** v. ☞ わざわざ～する

The heron was sure that a big, fat fish would come soon. She waited beside the stream, but only small fish appeared.[1]

As she waited, the sun rose [2] into the sky. The water became warm and all the small fish swam away. The heron was hungry, but she could only find a tiny snail.[3]

"I had so many choices [4] before," said the heron, "but I was too proud and hard to please. Now I have nothing to eat at all."

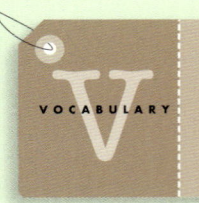

---

**VOCABULARY**

1. **appear** v. ☞ 現れる
2. **rise** v. (rise-rose-risen) ☞ 昇る
3. **snail** n. ☞ カタツムリ
4. **choice** n. ☞ 選択肢

*The Proud Heron* **高慢なサギ** | 103

### 訳：高慢なサギ

　昔、高慢なサギがいました。サギは、世界中で自分がいちばん賢く美しいと思っていました。
　ある朝、サギは小川のほとりに立ち、水をのぞき込みます。サギは、朝食用に大きく丸々とした魚がほしいと思いました。
「ここにはたくさん魚がいるわね」とサギ。
「でも、私には小さすぎる。いちばん大きく最高級の魚しか私にはふさわしくないもの！」
　ちょうどそのとき、岸辺に大きめの魚が泳いできました。それでもまだサギは興味を示しません。サギは言いました。
「こんなに小さな魚のために、わざわざ私の口を開けたりするものですか！」

　サギは、すぐに大きく丸々とした魚が来ると信じていました。しかし、小川のほとりで待っても、小さな魚が姿を現すだけです。
　待っている間に、空に太陽が上りました。水は温かくなり、小さな魚たちはみな泳ぎ去ってしまいました。サギはお腹が空きましたが、小さなカタツムリしか見つけられません。
「今までたくさんのチャンスがあったのに」
とサギは言いました。
「プライドが高く偏屈すぎたわ。もう食べるものが何もない」

# The Man Who Loved Money
# 守錢奴

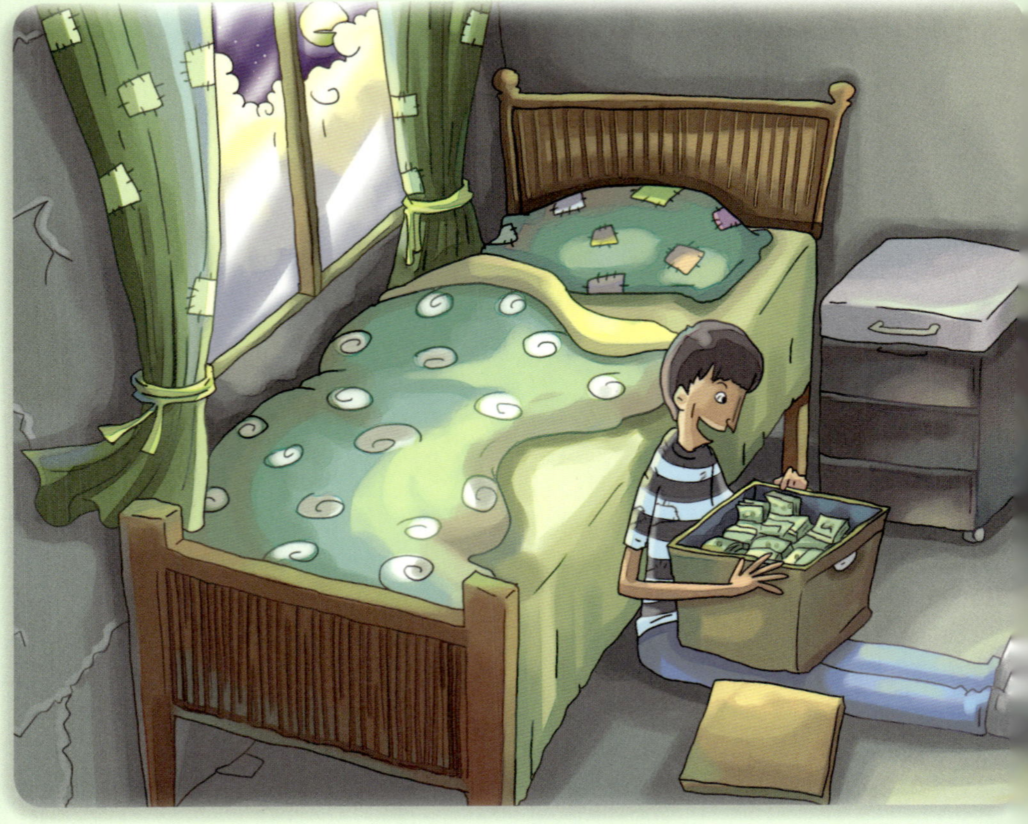

Once upon a time, there was a man who loved money. He loved it so much that he wouldn't spend any of the money he earned.❶ He wouldn't part with even a tiny bit.

This stingy❷ man didn't buy new clothes. Instead, he wore old clothes that he found in the garbage. He didn't buy food, either, and he became skinnier❸ and skinnier.

He put all the money that he saved❹ in a box and hid it under his bed. Every night, he opened the box and looked at all his money.

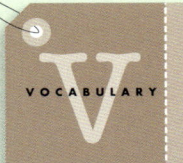

---

**VOCABULARY**

1. **earn** v. ☞ 稼ぐ
2. **stingy** adj. ☞ けちな
3. **skinny** adj. ☞ 痩せこけた
4. **save** v. ☞ 貯金する

One night, the man looked in the box and the money was gone! Someone had stolen[1] it! "I've been robbed!"[2] he shouted. "My precious[3] money is gone!" He lay down on the bed and cried and cried.

The neighbors[4] heard him and came over to see what was wrong. When they heard the story, one neighbor said, "Don't cry over your money. You never used it anyway. Fill the box with paper and imagine[5] it is money. It will do you just as much good."

1. **steal** v.(steal-stole-stolen) ☞ 盗む
2. **rob** v. ☞ 〜から奪う
3. **precious** adj. ☞ 大事な
4. **neighbors** n. ☞ 近所の人、隣人
5. **imagine** v. ☞ 想像する

*The Man Who Loved Money* 守錢奴 | 109

The Man Who Loved Money

### 訳：守銭奴

　昔、あるところにお金の大好きな男がいました。あまりにもお金が好きだったため、稼いだお金を少しも使いません。ほんのわずかなお金さえ手放そうとしませんでした。

　このケチ男は新しい服も買いません。そのかわり、ゴミの中から見つけた古着を着ていました。男は食料も買わなかったため、どんどんやせていきました。

　男は、貯めたお金を箱の中にすべて入れ、それをベッドの下に隠していました。毎晩、男は箱を開き、全財産をながめました。

　ある夜、男が箱の中を見ると、お金が消えています！　誰かが盗んだのです！
「盗まれた！」
と男は叫びました。
「僕の大事なお金がなくなってしまった！」
　男はベッドに横たわり、泣き続けました。
　隣人たちがその声を聞きつけ、何が起きたのか見にやってきました。話を聞くと、１人の隣人が言いました。
「自分のお金のことを嘆くんじゃない。どちらにせよ、君はそのお金を使わなかった。箱を紙で一杯にして、それが金だと想像するんだ。君にとっては同じようなものだろう」

**【ことわざ】**「宝の持ち腐れ」

# Danger Signs
# 危険信号

Once upon a time, there was an old lion. He was very slow, and it was difficult ❶ for him to catch any animals. When he did catch one, it always got away. He was too weak to hold onto them.

Then he had an idea! He told all the other animals that he was sick. Then he lay down in a cave ❷ and waited. When the other animals came to visit him, he leaped ❸ up and ate them.

**VOCABULARY**

1. **difficult** adj. ☞ 難しい
2. **cave** n. ☞ 洞穴、洞窟
3. **leap** v. ☞ 飛び跳ねる

*Danger Signs* **危険信号**

One day, an old and wise fox walked past the entrance ❶ to the cave. He called out to the lion and asked him how he was. "Bad," answered the hungry lion. "Why don't you come in and visit me?"

But the wise fox sensed ❷ danger. He had noticed that there were many tracks ❸ going into the cave and none at all coming back out. "No, thanks," said the wise fox. "I have lived to be very old because I always see the signs of danger before it is too late."

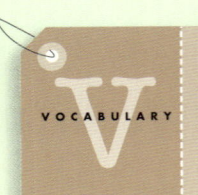

**VOCABULARY**

1. **entrance** n. ☞ 入り口
2. **sense** v. ☞ 〜を感知する
3. **track** n. ☞ 足跡

*Danger Signs* 危険信号

Danger Signs

訳：危険信号

　昔々、年老いたライオンがいました。ライオンの動きはとてもゆっくり。どんな動物もなかなか捕まえられません。ようやく捕えても、いつも逃げられてしまいます。力が弱く、つかんでいることもできなかったのです。
　そのとき、ある考えがひらめきました！　ライオンは自分が病気であることをほかの動物たちすべてに伝えました。そして洞窟に横たわり、待ちました。ほかの動物たちが訪ねてくると、飛びかかり食べてしまいました。

　ある日、賢い老ギツネが洞窟の入口の前を通りかかりました。ライオンに呼びかけ、どんな具合かたずねると、お腹をすかせたライオンは「良くない」と答えました。
「こっちに入ってきて、私を見舞ってくれないか」
　しかし、賢いキツネは危険を察しました。キツネは、洞窟の中に入っていく足跡はたくさんあるのに、出てきた足跡がまったくないことに気づいていたのです。
「いいや、結構」
　賢いキツネは言いました。
「私はこの歳になるまで生きてきた。それは、手遅れになる前に、いつも危険信号を見つけてきたからじゃよ」

　　　　　　　　　　　　　　【ことわざ】「亀の甲より年の功」
　　　　　　　　　　　　　　　　　　　　「霜を履みて堅氷到る」

# The Deer at the Pond
# 池のシカ

There once lived a deer who had large, strong antlers.❶ The antlers protected the deer from attacks, so enemies❷ left him alone.

One day, the deer went to a pond to drink. The water was like a mirror. When the deer looked at his big antlers in the water, he was proud. "I look like a king," he said, "and this forest is my kingdom."

Then he noticed something else. "My legs are slender❸ and my feet are small," he said. "They look so weak. I hate them."

**VOCABULARY**

1. **antler** n. ☞ [雄ジカの] 枝角
2. **enemy** n. ☞ 敵
3. **slender** adj. ☞ か細い

*The Deer at the Pond* 池のシカ

While the deer was complaining,❶ a wolf appeared at the pond. When the deer saw him, he ran toward the trees. The wolf quickly ran after him.

The deer was a fast runner and reached the trees first, but then his large antlers got stuck in some branches. When the wolf caught up to him, the deer cried out with regret.❷

"I admired ❸ my antlers, but they are the cause ❹ of my troubles. My legs and feet could have saved me, but I hated them. I didn't appreciate what was truly valuable!"

**VOCABULARY**

1. **complain** v. ☞ 不満を言う
2. **regret** n. ☞ 後悔
3. **admire** v. ☞ 〜を称賛する
4. **cause** n. ☞ 原因

*The Deer at the Pond* 池のシカ | 121

### 訳：池のシカ

　昔、大きくて強い角をもったシカがいました。角はシカを攻撃から守ったため、敵は誰もいなくなりました。
　ある日、シカは池に水を飲みに行きました。水は鏡のようです。シカは水に映った大きな角を見て自慢に思いました。
「王様のようだ」
とシカは言いました。
「この森はおれの王国だ」
　そのとき、シカは別のことに気づきます。
「おれの脚は細く、足は小さい」
とシカは言いました。
「とても弱々しく見える。いやだな」

　シカが愚痴をこぼしていると、池にオオカミが現れました。シカはオオカミを見ると、林に向かって走っていきました。オオカミはすぐにシカを追いかけます。
　シカの足は速く、先に林にたどり着きますが、そのとき、大きな角が枝にひっかかってしまいました。オオカミが追いつくと、シカは後悔して泣きました。
　「自分の角にほれぼれしていたけれど、これこそやっかいの原因だ。足はおれを助けてくれたのに嫌っていた。おれは本当に価値あるものに感謝していなかったんだ」

# The Fisherman and the Little Fish
# 漁師と小さな魚

The Fisherman and the Little Fish 漁師と小さな魚 | 123

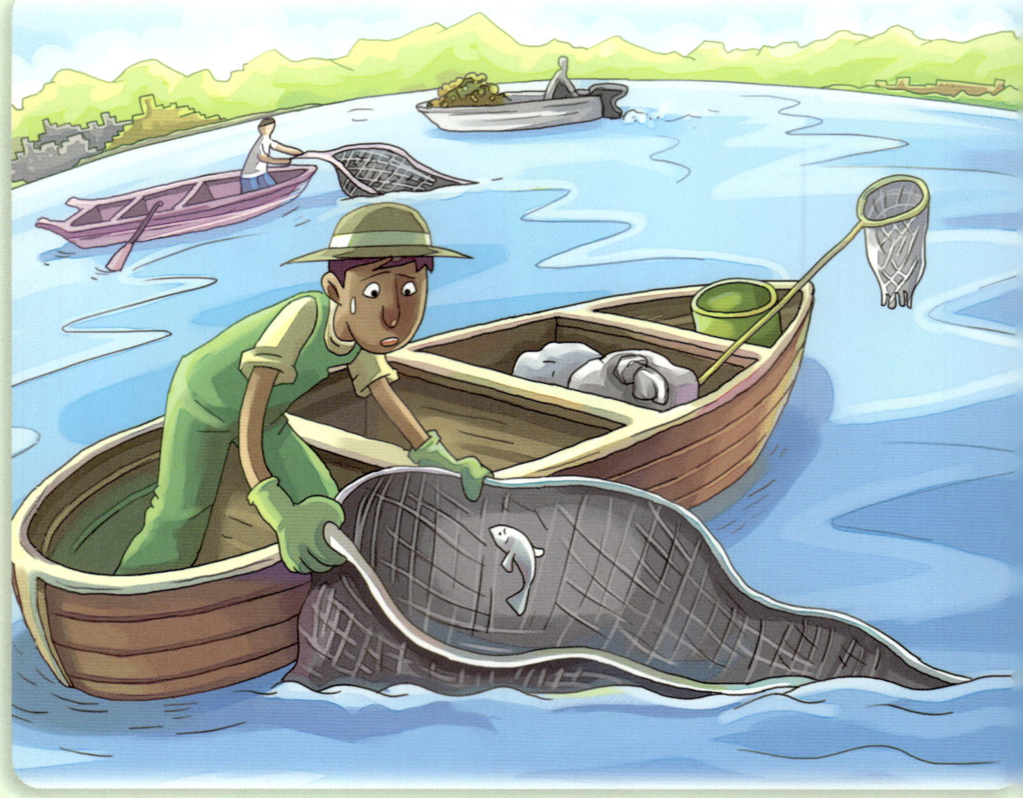

There once was a fisherman ❶ who lived in a little house by the ocean. He fished every day to feed his family. One day, he caught nothing except one small fish. "This isn't much," thought the fisherman, "but it's better than nothing."

The little fish hopped ❷ around in the net and cried out to the fisherman. "Please return ❸ me to the water!" he said. "I'm too small to be a good dinner. Someday, I'll be big and fat. You could catch me then and feed your family for a week!"

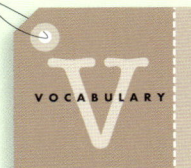

---

**VOCABULARY**

1. **fisherman** n. ☞ 漁師
2. **hop** v. ☞ ピョンピョン跳ぶ
3. **return** v. ☞ 〜を返す

*The Fisherman and the Little Fish* **漁師と小さな魚**

The fisherman listened as the fish spoke. He knew his family would love a big, fat fish, but he also knew that the ocean was very big. If he threw the fish back, he would never find it again.

"Little fish," he said, "I would be a fool❶ to put you back. You'll only be a small meal for my family, but at least they will have food. I cannot feed them with silly dreams!"

Appreciate❷ the small things that you have. Don't give them up to chase impossible things.

**VOCABULARY**

1. **fool** n. ☞ 愚か者
2. **appreciate** v. ☞ 〜をありがたく思う

*The Fisherman and the Little Fish* 漁師と小さな魚

### 訳：漁師と小さな魚

　昔、海辺の小さな家に住む1人の漁師がいました。漁師は、家族を養うため、毎日、漁をしました。ある日、小さな魚を1匹しか捕まえることができませんでした。
「これじゃ足りない」
　漁師は考えました。
「でも、何もないよりましだ」
　その小さな魚は、網中を飛び跳ね、漁師に頼みました。
「私を水に返してください！」
　魚は言います。
「私は、晩ご飯のごちそうには小さすぎます。いつか私は大きく太るでしょう。そのとき私を捕まえれば、あなたの家族を1週間は養えるはずです！」

　漁師は、魚が話すのを聞いていました。漁師は、家族が大きく丸々とした魚が好きなことを知っています。でも、海はとても大きいことも知っています。もし魚を海に帰せば、2度と見つけることはできないでしょう。
　「小魚よ」
と漁師は言いました。
「お前を放したら、僕は愚か者だ。お前は僕の家族にとってわずかな食事にしかならないが、少なくとも食料は手にできる。おろかな夢で家族を食べさせることはできないんだよ！」
　今ある小さなことに感謝しましょう。不可能なことを追いかけるためにその小さなことを手放してはいけないのです。

# Index

索引

## a

| | |
|---|---|
| act | 60 |
| admire | 120 |
| advice | 24 |
| alone | 71 |
| angry | 90 |
| antler | 118 |
| appear | 102 |
| appreciate | 126 |
| arrive | 48 |
| avoid | 13 |

## b

| | |
|---|---|
| beak | 23 |
| beat | 53 |
| beside | 48 |
| bother | 101 |
| bottom | 83 |
| branch | 53 |
| bright | 23 |
| bundle | 17 |

## c

| | |
|---|---|
| case | 97 |
| catch | 89 |
| cause | 120 |
| cave | 112 |
| certainly | 97 |
| chase | 89 |
| choice | 102 |
| clear | 72 |
| colorful | 23 |
| complain | 120 |
| crop | 41 |
| crow | 23 |

## d

| | |
|---|---|
| decision | 60 |
| defeat | 78 |
| demand | 94 |
| desert | 72 |
| deserve | 101 |
| difficult | 112 |
| dig | 35 |
| distance | 42 |
| dream | 37 |
| dry | 84 |

## e

| | |
|---|---|
| earn | 107 |
| emperor | 29 |
| enemy | 118 |
| enjoy | 54 |
| entrance | 114 |
| extra | 66 |

## f

| | |
|---|---|
| fail | 18 |
| fall into | 59 |
| fault | 90 |
| feather | 23 |
| field | 37 |
| fight | 17 |

| | |
|---|---|
| fisherman | 125 |
| flatter | 24 |
| fool | 126 |
| foolish | 60 |

## g
| | |
|---|---|
| gently | 54 |
| give ~ a second thought | 59 |
| glad | 84 |
| grab | 42 |
| grateful | 41 |

## h
| | |
|---|---|
| hardworking | 11 |
| harvest | 35 |
| heal | 94 |
| heavy | 65 |
| heron | 101 |
| hold onto | 54 |
| hop | 125 |

## i
| | |
|---|---|
| imagine | 108 |
| increase | 13 |
| intelligent | 29 |
| interested | 101 |

## j
| | |
|---|---|
| join | 48 |
| joke | 72 |
| judge | 97 |
| juicy | 37 |

## k
| | |
|---|---|
| kingdom | 29 |

## l
| | |
|---|---|
| land | 78 |
| laugh | 76 |
| leap | 112 |
| lesson | 18 |
| lift | 24 |
| load | 11 |

## m
| | |
|---|---|
| mad | 89 |
| master | 89 |
| mistake | 66 |
| mosquito | 76 |

## n
| | |
|---|---|
| neighbor | 108 |
| no matter how | 17 |
| no use | 54 |

## o
| | |
|---|---|
| on purpose | 11 |
| once upon a time | 71 |
| outside | 83 |

## p
| | |
|---|---|
| path | 71 |
| pay | 47 |
| perfect | 47 |
| place | 48 |
| praise | 90 |
| precious | 108 |
| pretend | 31 |
| price | 47 |
| promise | 97 |

## r
| | |
|---|---|
| realize | 66 |

| | |
|---|---|
| regret | 120 |
| repay | 42 |
| return | 125 |
| reward | 37 |
| rise | 102 |
| rob | 108 |
| run away | 60 |

## s

| | |
|---|---|
| salt | 11 |
| save | 107 |
| scared | 31 |
| seller | 47 |
| sense | 114 |
| serve | 65 |
| service | 90 |
| shore | 53 |
| sight | 94 |
| skinny | 107 |
| slender | 118 |
| slip | 11 |
| snail | 102 |
| sob | 84 |
| soon | 65 |
| sponge | 13 |
| spread | 41 |
| steal | 108 |
| stick | 17 |
| still | 72 |
| stingy | 107 |
| stone | 42 |
| straw | 17 |
| stream | 101 |
| strong | 18 |
| style | 31 |
| succeed | 18 |

| | |
|---|---|
| suddenly | 66 |
| sum | 94 |
| survive | 83 |
| swindler | 29 |

## t

| | |
|---|---|
| terribly | 59 |
| thin | 17 |
| thirsty | 59 |
| tiny | 78 |
| toward | 76 |
| track | 114 |
| trap | 41 |
| travel | 71 |
| treasure | 35 |
| trick | 13 |
| trouble | 72 |
| trust | 24 |
| turn | 54 |

## u

| | |
|---|---|
| underwear | 31 |

## v

| | |
|---|---|
| vase | 83 |
| vine | 35 |
| vineyard | 35 |

## w

| | |
|---|---|
| waste | 84 |
| wave | 53 |
| weak | 18 |
| web | 78 |
| weight | 13 |
| well | 59 |

# LiveABC

　株式会社 Live ABC は、台湾の e-Learning プログラムにおいてトップレベルの実績を誇っている大手出版社です。最先端の IT 技術と経験豊富な技術者と語学教師及び編集スタッフによって、インタラクティブマルチメディア語学学習教材の研究開発に取り組んでいます。

　現在、英語を筆頭に中国語、日本語、韓国語などの語学学習教材を、書籍や、CD-ROM、スマートフォン対応のアプリで提供しています。

ホームページ（英語）：http://www.liveabc.com

| | |
|---|---|
| カバーデザイン | 土岐 晋二（デザイン事務所フラクタル） |
| 本文デザイン／DTP | 土岐 晋二（デザイン事務所フラクタル） |
| CD ナレーション | Jack Merluzzi |
| | Carolyn Miller |
| | 城内 美登理 |

音読 CD BOOK ②
やさしい英語で読む　世界のおとぎ話　～ Bedtime Stories ～　BEST 20
平成 23 年（2011 年）　2 月 10 日発売　初版第 1 刷発行
平成 24 年（2012 年）　4 月 10 日　　　　第 3 刷発行

編　者　Live ABC
発行人　福田富与
発行所　有限会社　J リサーチ出版
　　　　〒 166-0002　東京都杉並区高円寺北 2-29-14-705
　　　　電話 03 (6808) 8801（代）　FAX 03 (5364) 5310
　　　　編集部 03 (6808) 8806
　　　　http://www.jresearch.co.jp
印刷所　（株）シナノ パブリッシング プレス

ISBN978-4-86392-049-1　禁無断転載。なお、乱丁・落丁はお取り替えいたします。
Copyright ©2011 LiveABC Interactive Corporation
Japanese translation copyright ©2011 J-Research Press. Japanese edition. All Rights Reserved.